USING EXCEL AS A BEGINNER

A guide on how to use Excel in Computer

BONIFACE BENEDICT

DEDICATION

This book is dedicated to all computer professionals all around the world

TABLE OF CONTENTS

USING EXCEL AS A BEGINNER i
    A guide on how to use Excel in Computer i
    BONIFACE BENEDICT i
    DEDICATION ii
    ACKNOWLEDGEMENT v
Introduction..1
Chapter One 4
    Basic Fundamentals..4
        Launching Excel for the first time.....................................4
    What's a worksheet?..8
    Utilizing the Quick Access Toolbar 9
    Here's how to change view of Workbook............................13
    How to Split Windows 16
    Here's how to work with an Existing Workbook 20
    How to navigate data with Go To Command......................21
    How to navigate a worksheet 22
Chapter Two 26
    Performing tasks with Excel 26

Making workbook from scratch 27

How to save your Workbook 30

How to make Input and Edit Data in a Worksheet 40

Chapter Three 55

Using fundamental Formulas in Excel 55

Interpreting and displaying Formulas 55

How to Understand Order of Operators 58

Applying Cell References in Formulas 61

Applying cell ranges in formula 69

Applying External Cell references 76

Chapter Four 82

Charts and pictures 82

Chart 82

Pictures or Graphics 88

ACKNOWLEDGEMENT

This is to acknowledge Mr. Charles for his encouragement. And I also thank my friends; Jane, Stella for their encouragement towards making sure that this book was a success.

Introduction

This is great! I introduce you to a step by step guide on how to use Excel in your computer, the latest edition. With this book, you can be able to build your skills as you proceed in learning specialized methods of input and output of data cells. Or if you seem to be a pro in some parts, you can simply surpass all "I-know-it" topics and begin to have a ready guidance on the topics that you might be a novice in.

This book would solidly cover all basic techniques, from creating, editing, formatting and printing of worksheets. In addition, this book would also expose you to the fundamentals of creating data lists, charting and performing appropriate data analytics. And please do keep this in mind that this book would touch on the easiest ways to get a few things done, also including the essentials. Albeit, I don't attempt to be intense with techniques like, data analysis, charting, and data lists not comparing them in a definitive way in the manner we would be handling spreadsheet data. This book would generally focus on spreadsheets and that's because this tool is what most consumers create with Excel.

Who has a right to use this book?

Excel for beginners is specifically designed for use as a learning and reference resource by both home and business users, who desire to utilize excel so as to manage data, make useful analyses, discover insights into particular operations in all spheres of business, utilizing all business intelligence analytic tools and giving a breakdown on visualizing contents. This book's aim is to make beginners become partial pros in the near future.

Basic approach

The book is categorized into parts for emphasis and in some areas succinctly describes general Excel skill sets. Each part is divided into chapters, in which it would also be distinctly passing the required information. I would be applying the expository technique of learning in some areas, which would be followed by very comprehensive methods. When done with learning Excel, you can also purchase the other book series which would give more emphasis on Excel tables. It is titled, *How to use Excel tables for dummies 2020.*

Chapter One
Basic Fundamentals

Launching Excel for the first time, well you've got to know the nitty-gritty stuff of this program. Excel is a powerful electronic or computer spreadsheet program, which is designed to automate accounting work, perform many tasks and not forgetting the best part, to organize all your data problems. It is also designed to analyze information, visualize data in a spreadsheet and perform calculations. In addition, this application includes charting features and database.

Launching Excel for the first time

Here are 3 simple steps that'll be as easy as making

milkshake for morning breakfast. You also have to note that this is specifically for Windows 10 users:

i. Direct the pointer of your computer and click the **Windows icon** on the left bottom corner

ii. Immediately that's done, an interface pops up and all apps are shown

iii. Scroll and look for Excel, when it's seen click it.

iv. Click the blank workbook on display, a blank workbook opens and the worksheet name *Sheet* is immediately displayed.

Excel is known to open to a list of templates to work with, and in most cases you either open a previous file or choose blank workbook. A workbook is sort of like a physical book with numerous pages.

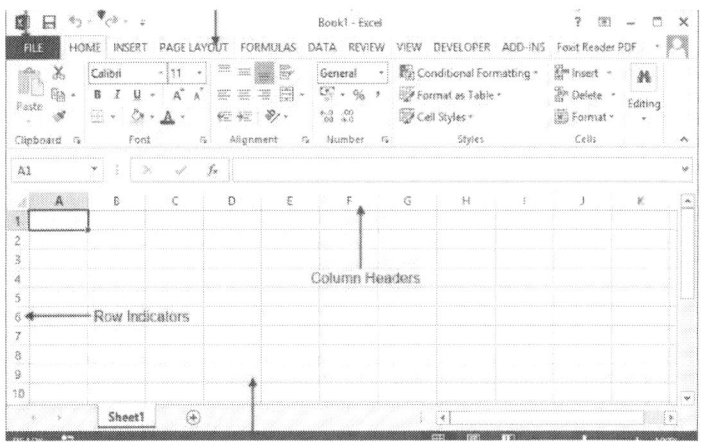

The program name and the file name appears together in the title bar at the top of screen, this gives users the ease in identifying their files after a specified instruction. As observed most times, the computer loves to help so to make the user have easy reach of his or her files, the computer would have to save such commands or instructions given by the user with a temporary title, for instance we have, Book 1, Book 2, Book 3 and it goes on and on; this is done until the user, which is you saves the workbook with a preferred name. You can name the workbook with absolutely any name, even a pen name. For example, **"Paula starlight document"**.

The new workbook is featured with one worksheet, which is called "worksheet 1" by default. Kind of similar to the first page in a book; if you get the hint. This is where you type in your information.

If a workbook has more worksheets or pages, it is advised you use the sheet tabs that are located just a bit above the status bar and are known with name tags as, "Sheet 1, Sheet 2, Sheet 3." You can also place titles or name your worksheet after placing contents/information, this is done so as to easily identify information placed in the worksheet or page, and further proceed to add worksheet with a New sheet button; which is indicated with this symbol or toolbar (+).

Please note: If perhaps this is your first time in using Excel and you do use it often, I advise you pin the application to the start menu. This would be really helpful so as to avoid the stress of looking for the app. To do this, search for all apps menu, right click the app name. Immediately you do this an instruction would pop-up to make a choice, you can now choose Pin to Start. You can also choose "More" and then pin the app to taskbar. This allows you click the icon in the windows taskbar, situated just at the bottom of the screen so as to start Excel.

What's a worksheet? A worksheet is a grid which is composed of cells, grids and columns. In a worksheet, each column begins at the top of the worksheet and goes below, which is identified by a letter. Each row begins at the left edge of the worksheet and proceeds to the right, which is known by a number. Each cell or box on the right grid is known by the intersection of a row and a column. This makes the first box or cell in an open worksheet to be indicated as AI. All you have to do is type into the active cell, outlined by a bold, distinct box. This is called the highlighted or current cell, and that's because it is currently worked with by the user.

Utilizing the Quick Access Toolbar: Also called onscreen tools because of the ease of identification onscreen, just above the worksheet. It is here to give you easy and fast access to basic tools, especially tools you use more often in a given Excel operation. It is easily located at the left side corner of the title bar, just above the ribbon. However, you have the freedom to move the toolbar below the ribbon, especially if you desire to have it closer to your work point or area. You can remove and add commands to and from the toolbar so that it has only those commands you use more commonly. You also have the liberty to learn how to use basic ScreenTips, which are small, onscreen boxes that show descriptive text when you rest the pointer on a control or command.

Here's how to use it;

    a. Direct your pointer and point to each icon of your choice on the Quick Access Toolbar. When that's done, read the description that's displayed as a ScreenTip.

    b. On the right side of the onscreen tool, click the drop-down arrow. From the drop-down list, choose Open. The Open icon is immediately added to the Onscreen or Quick Access Toolbar. You can proceed to perform other functions so that such function can be added to the Quick Access Toolbar. For instance, click the drop-down arrow again, and choose Email or Print Preview from the drop-down list.

c. Next up, you right-click anywhere on the onscreen toolbar and then choose "Show Quick Access Toolbar below the Ribbon."

d. Then you right-click the Home tab and click "collapse ribbon". Now in this part, only the tabs are shown thereby increasing the workspace area.

e. Right-click the home tab once more, and select "collapse ribbon" so as to uncheck the option and make the instructions visible.

f. On the right-side of the Quick access toolbar, which is now shown below the ribbon, click the drop-down arrow. And click the "show above the ribbon" from the drop-down list.

g. Right-click the "Open" instruction or command and choose "Remove from Quick Access Toolbar."

h. While on the right-side of the Quick Access toolbar, click the drop-down arrow and also click "Quick print" so as to remove the checkmark from the menu, and also remove the "Quick Print" icon from the onscreen toolbar.

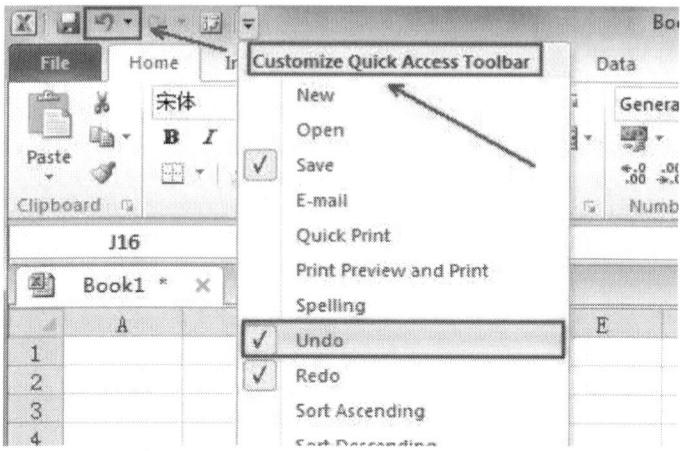

Here's how to change view of Workbook

Located at the ribbon, the "view tab" holds and executes instructions for controlling displays of the displayed workbook. You can do a variety of stuff to sort all your needs just by the use of this view tab. For example, you can execute and arrange new windows, split windows for side by side displays that fits comfortably with your immediate need.

How to change the Workbook View

Some set or groups on the ribbon tabs do have a directive pointer in their lower-length corner, which is called a "dialog box launcher." Clicking the directive pointer opens a task pane containing more alternatives for that particular set or group of instructions.

   a. Click the home tab to execute
   b. Choose cell A1 so as to make it active. Then type 358 and click the tab
   c. Now move to the lower-right corner of the font group and click the "Task pane Launcher Arrow". The *Format cells* task pane box would have the appropriate commands that you must strictly follow. Most cases the default font for Excel is Calibri, eleven point, without italic or bold
   d. You'll also notice that the font tab of the task pane is operational or active. Make a scroll down in the font list and click "the font you like, for example,

Cambria," and then you click OK. This automatically registers the cell. And Cell B1 is operational now

e. Type in 358 in this cell and then press or click the Tab. If you'll notice, there'll be a difference between this present number and the one you entered previously in cell A1

f. Next up, click the view tab

g. In the workbook views group click "Page Layout". With this view active, you can see the margins, and particular places the pages break and you can also add a header or footer, to give it that professional notch.

h. In the Workbook Views group, press "Normal" to return the worksheet to default. This would no longer display, footers, headers, page breaks and rulers.

How to Split Windows

Most times, working worksheets done by you may contain lots of data, and in this case you can only see a small part of the worksheet in Excels page and Normal layout or structured views. With the split command you can overcome or correct such limitation and that's by viewing the worksheet in 2 panes or 4 quadrants.

When done with issuing this command, you can proceed in using the scroll bars on the right-bottom part of the window so as to show different sections of the worksheet being active at the same time. This helps as it gives you the opportunity to contrast and compare data or see the influence a change in one part of the worksheet might have on a distant part of the same worksheet. This exercise is strictly on how to split Excel window and also making the best use of the tools as provided, for instance using the scroll bars to view different sections of a worksheet.

It would also be good if you practice making input or entering data into the cells of the split windows, and you also have a good knowledge on how to disable the split to return to single-window view.

Please, to have a thorough follow on the idea of this exercise without causing any form of disorganization, I'll prefer you use the worksheet left open in the previous exercise if perhaps, you did or you can as well type 358 in cells A1 and B1 in a new workbook.

a. The first step in splitting the windows, click cell F1 to make it operational

b. The view tab is displayed, now proceed to click "Split." You'll immediately notice that the screen is split vertically in 2 different panes.

c. For the horizontal scroll bar of the right pane, you hold down the "Right Arrow," until you can see cell AA1. You'll also notice that in this part, cells A1 and B1 is still shown in the left pane.

d. Click the "Split" once more, and you'll observe immediately you do this the screen is no longer split.

e. Next up, click in cell A17 and proceed to click "Split". With this, the screen is automatically split horizontally in 2 entirely different panes.

f. Click the "Split" again and the screen returns to its normalcy, that is to say, it no longer has a split screen.

g. Click cell F14 and click split. The screen is quickly divided into 4 panes.

h. Select the lower-right quadrant by clicking any cell in the quadrant pane, and then you can proceed by scrolling down to display row forty.

i. In cell H40, type in 238 and press enter. With this the data you entered in cells A1 and B1 should become visible at this moment, along with what you entered in cell H40.

How great! You've fully learnt the fundamentals of Excel, and please note that the split command is very useful when it comes to comparing various parts of a long worksheet.

Here's how to work with an Existing Workbook

As a computer-user, you may need to update your workbook from time to time and that's because, existing data has been changed by a new input of data. Most workers would have to open an existing workbook, make updates and then save the workbook to be revised periodically. More often than not, files are made by a single person and then used and updated from time to time by other colleagues.

You also have to know that file name must indicate the goal or purpose of such type of data as contained in the file. A descriptive file name is necessary as it enables you to retrieve and locate files more quickly. File names have a maximum of 255 characters, which includes the filename extension. Nevertheless, as observed in most working environments, workers use more of shorter descriptive filenames that clearly gives an indication of contents in the workbook.

How to navigate data with Go To Command

Perhaps you're the kind that works with large volumes of data, and I guess it would be rather too tasking to begin to scroll up and down so as to check where you had stopped making inputs and proceed with the task at hand. Well, no worries with the Go To Command you have a clear shot and no hassles whatsoever. This command takes you to the particular points in the worksheet, which includes cell ranges and cells that you had named.

The steps;

Click the "File Tab" and click "Open", then you click "Browse". In the open task pane or dialog box select the location of your lesson 01 data files, for example, choose ***"We are the employee top secret"*** and then proceed to press "Open."

a) Choose cell A17

b) In the Name Box to the left side of the formula bar, choose A17

c) Remove A17 by deleting, and type "MedAssts", then click enter

d) Click cell M11

e) Proceed to the Home tab, in the Editing group, and select "Find and Select". Press "Go To". The Go To task pane is quickly displayed.

How to navigate a worksheet

Excel worksheet most times do contain more than sixteen thousand columns and a million rows. There are a variety of methods to move through worksheets that contain a variety of columns and rows. You can either use the scroll bars, mouse or the arrow keys to navigate through the used worksheet and if you desire to make inputs and perform a task with the worksheet, you can still use this tools as described.

Basically to make it simple for you, here are the steps;

First of all, click the "File Tab" and click "Open", then you click "Browse". In the open task pane or dialog box select the location of your lesson 01 data files, for example, choose **"We are the employee top secret"** and then proceed to press "Open."

- a) Click "Ctrl+End" to move to the end of the worksheet (cell D27)
- b) Click "Ctrl+Home" to move to the beginning of the worksheet (cell A1)
- c) Press in the "Name box", type A3 and then click "Enter" to quickly make the cell operative

d) Click "Ctrl+Down Arrow" to go immediately to the last row of data (cell A7)

Please, you also have to know that Ctrl+Arrow commands permits you to move to the beginning and end of ranges of data. While the worksheet title or name page, which covers all columns isn't included as part of the worksheet's data range

e) Click Ctrl+Right Arrow. Cell D27, indicated as the last column in the range of data, which becomes the active cell.

f) Click Ctrl+Down Arrow. The last possible row in the worksheet would be shown

g) Click Ctrl+Home

h) Use vertical scroll bar to navigate from the top to the end of the data set.

i) If your mouse does have a wheel button, then it would be appropriate to roll the wheel button forward and back to scroll through the worksheet.

j)

Chapter Two

Performing tasks with Excel

The toolbar in Excel contains a variety of tabs each related to specific types of tasks that helps you perform effectively in Excel. For the Home Tab it, which is located just above an active worksheet contains the commands or instructions that people use more often when making Excel documents.

Therefore having commands visibly at the work surface enables you the user to see briefly most tasks you wish to perform. Each tab contains sets of commands related to particular functions and tasks. Some commands have an arrow which is more associated with them, for instance button arrows are more associated with Find & select and

AutoSum. Which also indicates that in addition to the default tasks other alternatives are more or less available for the task. In similar terms, some of the groups have task panes that are combined with them. Pressing this shows additional instructions not shown on the toolbar. For instance, Number groups, Alignment, Font and Clipboard have combined task panes, while Cells, Editing and Styles do not have such.

Making workbook from scratch

Creating a new workbook is done by following this simple procedures, launch Excel and choose a blank workbook or another kind of template. If you work with Excel more often and want to know how to begin a workbook, perhaps when done with one, click the "File Tab", then proceed to click New and then click blank workbook. These worksheets often contains texts that describes all contents of the worksheet.

Steps on creating a workbook from scratch

First of launch Excel. This gives you a variety of options for either starting a workbook, using templates or taking a tour.

a) Click "Blank workbook" as shown on the window. And if you have just launched Excel, Book 1-Excel displays in the title bar at the top of the windows. You'll also have to know that a blank workbook is opened with A1 as the active cell.

b) In the cell A1, type "We Love Windows, Inc." This entry is going to be the basic title for the worksheet. You'll also note that when you type, the text displays in the cell and in the formula bar. The term formula bar would soon be explained shortly.

c) Click "Enter". The text is quickly entered into cell A1, but is shown as if it is flowing to B1.

d) In cell A2, type the initials you wish to work with, for example, "200 Fox road" and then click enter.

e) In cell A3, type the initials you wish to work with, for example, "Brooklyn, CH 234567" and you click enter.

f) Sometimes, you also need a quick work area to fully complete another task while you're in the middle of a workbook. In this case, you can open another workbook as a scratch area. The procedures are as follows, click "File Tab" and in the left pane, click "New". The different templates which are available is quickly shown.

g) In the backstage view press "Blank workbook". Immediately, a second Excel Workbook opens and "Book 2" is displayed in the title bar.

h) In cell A1, type in the words to be used or applied, for example, "Telegraph Messages" and then click enter.

i) For cell A2, type words to be used, for example, "Michelle Todd VA flight 345 arriving 6:00 AM" and proceed in clicking enter.

j) Press the "File Tab" so as to open Backstage View. For the left pane, press "Close" to close the telegraph messages workbook. Then proceed to the message box and press "Don't save".

How to save your Workbook

When desiring to save file for the first time, you'll be asked the following questions: what name will you give the file? Where do you want to save the file? This section would focus on answering these questions for at least two contrasting documents or files.

By definite default in all Windows office applications, files are saved to the file folder or if you wish to your OneDrive, and that depends on the settings specified during installation of the program.

Saving your workbook in your OneDrive

OneDrive is known as a cloud-based app that permits you to synchronize and store your documents so that you can obtain or retrieve them anywhere and share them with numerous people as desired by you. It is also a great place to store backup files of important files or more succinctly, documents. It also comes with updated versions of Microsoft Office and Windows. And you also have access to a free desktop app, which is also available for phones.

Please, do endeavor to use active workbook from previous practice.

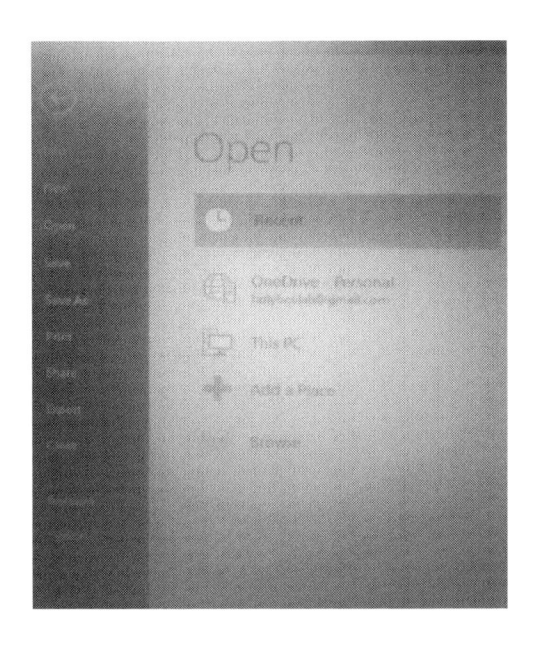

The steps;

1) Press "File Tab" and then press "Save As".

2) Proceed in the Backstage View, Under "Save As" and click your "OneDrive" account, then press a folder location with the pointer, which is located at the right pane. If you haven't signed in on OneDrive, it is advisable you do so.

3) Click the "New Folder" button in the "Save As" task pane.

4) In the "New folder" text box, type "My Excel lesson 2"; this helps to locate your document more quickly in the cloud, and immediately you press enter the folder is saved on OneDrive automatically.

5) Double-click the "Excel Lesson 2" symbol or icon so as to move the folder.

6) Make sure to keep the file with the same name or type 12 Kings Address solution in the file name box, and then press the "Save Button."

Saving your workbook in the File folder

It is advisable, you proceed with the active workbook as performed from the previous practice.

The steps;

1) Press the "File Tab" so as to open backstage view. Proceed to the left pane and press "Save As" to display the saving alternatives or options.

2) Double-click "This PC" to begin the "Save As" task pane.

3) For the navigation pane on the left corner, in the "Save As" task pane, click "Desktop". The desktop automatically becomes the new point or destination of your saved file.

4) In the "Save As" task pane, press "New Folder". A folder symbol or icon is shown with the words distinctly written, "New Folder" chosen.

5) Type in initials "Excel Lesson 2" and then proceed to click "Enter."

6) Press the "Open" button.

7) Then in the File name box, type in initials to be used by you, for example, "12 Kings Address Solution."

8) Press the "Save" button.

How to save workbook with a different Name

As always use active workbook from previous practice.

1) In cell A2, type initials, "12 Kings Crescent" and click the enter key.

2) In cell A3, type initials, "Austin, TX 3456" and then click the enter key.

3) Press the "File Tab" and in the left pane, press "Save As." With this the backstage view displays and indicates the current folder in the right pane is Excel Lesson 2 on your OneDrive, and that's because it was the folder that was last used to save the previous workbook.

4) Press "This PC" so as to return to the drive you had used before.

5) In the right pane, press "Excel Lesson 2."

6) Press in the "File name" box and click after "Kings" and then type "Landing" so the name reads "12 Kings Landing Address correction".

7) Press "Save". With this you have just made a new workbook by saving an existing workbook with a new name.

8) Press the "File Tab", and press "Save As" in the Left pane, then you press "Browse".

9) In the file name box, type "12 Kings Landing Address template correction".

10) In the Save As type box, press the drop-down arrow and select "Excel Template." Press the "Save" button.

PS: You also have to know that templates are saved in

another location entirely. This makes it easier for you to find and open the File, New option.

How to Save in Different File Formats

Please use the "12 Kings Landing Address correction" workbook from the previous practice or exercise, or you can type your address and name in a new workbook.

1) Press the "File Tab" and then press the "Export" key button.

2) Press the "Change File type" button. With this Excel would be able to explain the different document types.

3) Press the "Create PDF/XPS file or document" option.

4) In the right pane, click the "Create PDF/XPS" key button.

5) Proceed to the left navigation pane and press, "Desktop."

6) Double-click "Excel Lesson 2" to move to that specified folder.

7) When shown publish as PDF or XPS task pane, do ensure that the save as type list displays PDF.

8) Click or press "Publish".

9) The Web Browser opens with the PDF file shown.

10) Click Alt+F4 to end the browser.

11) If it's necessary to you, click Alt+Tab to return to Excel File.

You can now stop, end and leave the Excel open, so that we can perform the next task.

How to Save Workbook in previous Excel Style or Format

Well, you can launch the program here.

1) Located at the bottom of the left pane, press "Open Other Workbooks"

2) Then scroll down in the list of all recent documents in the right pane and press "12 Kings Landing Address correction".

3) Do observe carefully for any form of compatibility issues. Press the "File Tab", Press "Info", press "Check for issues" and then finally press "Check Compatibility". The Microsoft compatibility task pane quickly pops up and begins to actualize the requested instruction.

4) Now read the information in the **Compatibility Checker** task pane and then press "Ok".

5) Press the "File Tab", and press "Export", then further press "Change file Type". With this the backstage view displays the different file types.

6) Press "Excel 97-2003 workbook" and proceed to press "Save As".

7) In the document name box, press before "Solution", type "97-03" and press "Save".

8) Press the "File Tab" and then press "Close" to close the stated workbook or document.

9) Press the "File Tab" and then press "Open". The right stage in backstage view displays the last set of files that have been recently saved.

10) Then proceed the click the document you recently saved.

How to make Input and Edit Data in a Worksheet

Changing Column Width

You can use the existent file you're working with.

1) Hold mouse and move pointer between columns A and B, this would direct to the column markers just above the worksheet and immediately you do this the mouse pointer turns to a double-headed arrow.

2) Proceed to double-click the column marker between the A and B. With this the width of the column changes to the widest entry located in column A.

PS: If you desire to change the column width manually, all you have to do is point to the column marker which is between column A and B and drag the pointer left or right instead of double-clicking it.

3) Now you drag the double-headed arrow pointer between column B and C and do this till the screen Tip shows Width: 21 or something a little bit close

to this amount. When done with that release the mouse.

4) Save existing file. This action overwrites the previous version without the column width change.

How to enter Data in a Worksheet

Launch program and proceed in opening a new workbook

Here are the steps;

1) Press cell A1 and type "Kings Landing Plc" and then click "Enter. You'll notice that the active cell quickly moves to the next row that is to cell A2.

2) While in cell A2, type initials the nay initials your working with like, "Workers list" and then click "Enter".

3) Press the A4 and type "Name" and then click "Tab". You'll notice at this point that the cell is moving to the next column that is to cell B4.

Quick Resolution: If perhaps you type the wrong data, you can press the cell and retype entry data, in the following parts of this book you'll see how to edit text.

4) Type in "Extension" and then click "Enter". You'll notice that the active cell quickly moves to the 1st cell in the next row.

5) Next up, type in "Corey Hamilton" and then click "Tab".

6) Type in "202" and then click "Enter". With this Corey Hamilton's name looks short.

7) Press cell A5 and you'll notice that the full entry for Corey Hamilton shows in the formula bar.

8) Press cell A6 and type in "Paula Todd" and then proceed to click "Enter".

9) Type in "Sandra Bullock" and then click "Enter".

10) Type in "Jeffery Garden" and then click "Enter".

11) Save the workbook in Excel Lesson 2 folder in your computer as "12 Kings Landing Workers correction".

How to Edit Cell content

Here you'll have to open a new workbook.

1) Press cell A1 and type "Kings Landing" and then click "Enter". You'll notice the insertion point moves to cell A2 and nothing shows in the formula bar.

2) Press cell A1. You'll observe at this point the formula bar shows "Kings Landing ".

3) Press after "Kings Landing" in the formula bar and leave a space then type "plc" and then you proceed by clicking the "Tab". With this the insertion point moves to cell B1 and nothing shows in formula bar.

4) Press cell A1 and in the formula bar, double-click on "plc" to choose it. Type "plc" and then click "Enter".

5) Type in "Sales" and then click 'Enter".

6) Press cell A2 and proceed to press after "sales" in the formula bar.

7) Click "Home" and the insertion point moves to the starting point of the formula bar.

8) Type in "Monthly" and then proceed in clicking the spacebar. Press "Enter".

9) In cell A3, type in "February" and then click "Enter".

10) Press cell A3 and type "March", when done with that press "Enter". With that cell A3's present text disappears and March replaces January.

11) Press cell A3 and then press "Delete". With this the entry in A3 is immediately removed.

12) Just above row 1 and to the left of column A, press the 'Select All' key button. All cells on the worksheet would become selected.

13) Click "Delete" and all entries would be removed.

Overall check:

If you want to edit a cell all you have to do is double-click the cell and then type in the replacement text in the cell or to make it easy you can click the cell and hen press in the formula bar.

You have to know that when you are in edit mode, these are what you get;

- The edit indicator shows at the left end of the status bar
- The insertion point shows a vertical bar and other commands remain dormant or suspended.
- You can proceed in moving the insertion point by using the left and right pointer/arrow keys.

How to enter Dates

Open existing working document, that is, "12 Kings Landing…" from the data files.

1) Press cell B5 and type 2/5/2018 and then click "Enter".

2) Press cell B6 and type 2/5/18 and then click "Enter". The date is quickly entered in B6 as *2/5/2018* and the B7 becomes the active cell.

3) Type 5/24 and proceed in clicking "Enter". 24-May is entered in the cell. Press cell B7 and

observe 5/24/20XX (XX would have to represent the current year the computer is working with) shown in the formula bar.

4) If the year shown in the formula bar isn't 2018, press cell B7 and then click F2. Proceed to change the name to 2018 and then click "Enter".

5) In cell B8, type 5/25/18 and then click "Enter".

6) In cell B9, type May 26, 2018 and then click "Enter". With this 26-May-18 shows in the cell. If you made an input or entered date in an entirely different format than is specified or you entered something in the cell and removed or deleted it, your worksheet might not show the results described. With this, the date format in column B would not be consistent. Make sure to apply a consistent format in the next section.

7) In cell B9, type 5/5/18 and click "Enter". You'll observe that the value changes but the format still

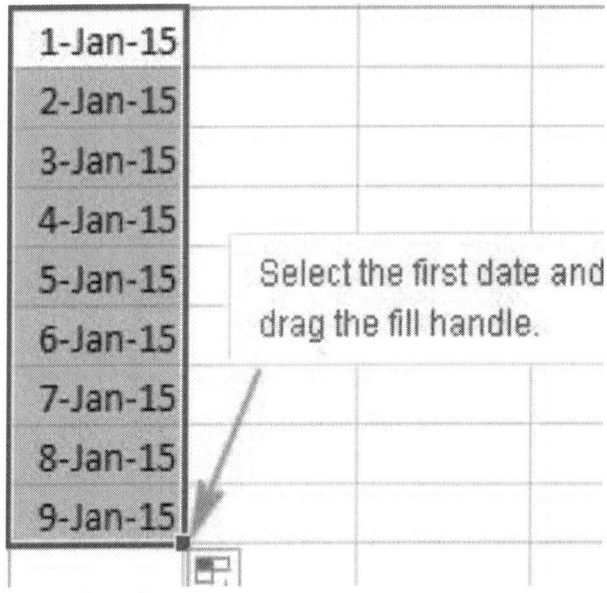

| 1-Jan-15 |
| 2-Jan-15 |
| 3-Jan-15 |
| 4-Jan-15 |
| 5-Jan-15 |
| 6-Jan-15 |
| 7-Jan-15 |
| 8-Jan-15 |
| 9-Jan-15 |

Select the first date and drag the fill handle.

remains the same.

8) Press the "Undo" button so as to return to the workbook.

Briefing on how to fill a series with Auto Fill

The program provides users Auto Fill alternatives that

automatically fills cells with formatting or data. To fill a new cell with required data that exists in adjacent cells, you'll have to use the Auto Fill basics either via command or the fill handle.

The fill handle can be identified as a small green square in the lower-right corner of a chosen range of cells.

A range is a set of adjacent cells that you choose so as to perform operations on all chosen cells. What to you refer to a range of cells, the 1st and the last cell are distinct by a colon. To apply the fill handle, point to the lower-right corner of the cell or range till the mouse pointer changes into a + (plus) symbol. Then proceed to click and drag the fill handle from range that contain data to the range or cell you want to fill with that data or you can have the program, Excel automatically continue to operate a variety or series of numbers and text, numbers, time periods, dates and text combinations all based on an established pattern.

Now to choose an interval for your series, type the 1st two entries, choose them, and then use the fill handle to expand the variety or series using the pattern of the 2 chosen cells.

How to fill a series with Autofill

Please proceed to use the workbook from previous lessons

1) Choose the range C4:H4. May would be in the 1st cell.
2) Proceed to the Home tab, in the editing group, press the "Fill" Button and the Fill menu is shown.
3) Form the menu, press "Right". The contents of C4 (May) are filled into all cells.
4) Press the "Undo" button.
5) Choose the range C9:C13 and then press the "Fill" button. Select "Down" and the content of C9 is copied into the 4 additional range.

6) Press the "Undo" button.

7) Press cell C4 and point to the fill handle in the lower-right corner of the cell. Drag it to the E4 and release the pointer. The Auto Fill alternative or options button shows next to the range and May through July are shown.

8) Click cell C5 and point to the fill handle. Drag it to C9 and release pointer. All numbers change to $275,000 in column C. the Auto Fill options button is shown near the lower-right corner of the chosen range.

9) Press the "Auto Fill options" button and select "Fill Formatting only" from the list that is shown. All he number immediately return to their previous values and are formatted with dollar commas and symbols.

10) Now repeat steps 8 and 9 for the range B5:B9.

11) Press cell A9, and then drag the fill handle down to A15, with this Ryan Calafato's name is repeated.

12) Press the "Undo" button so as to return the spreadsheet.

13) Save the workbook as "12 Kings Landing sales solution."

How to fill a series with Flash Fill

Open the file name 02 customers or whatever you had named it from the data files.

1) Please observe the customer list in column A, which includes the last name followed by a comma and then the 1st name. You want to make distinct columns for the 1st and the last names.

2) Choose cell B2 in the 1st name column.

3) Type "Alice" and click 'Enter".

4) In cell B3, type Ai to start the next 1st name. Aidan. Excel in this minute would presume you want to enter the rest of the 1st names in column B and it shows a preview of the results.

5) Click "Enter" to accept the suggestion. With this the remaining 1st names fill down the column. Also observe that Excel also would include middle initials for those names that include them.

6) Choose cell C2 in the last name column.

7) Type "Ciccu" and then click "Enter".

8) In cell C3, type "De" to begin the next last name, Delaney. The program would guess that you want to enter the rest of the last name in column C and it shows you a preview of the results.

Chapter Three

Using fundamental Formulas in Excel

Interpreting and displaying Formulas

1) Click cell A1.

2) Type in "=7*9*3/4-2" and click "Enter". With this you had just entered a formula.

PS: All formulas should be typed without spaces, but if you do type spaces, Excel removes them when you click "Enter".

3) Press cell A1. You'll observe that the result of the formula shows in the cell, but the family itself shows in the formula bar.

4) Now double-click cell A1. The formula shows in both the active cell and the formula bar. In this mode you can edit the formula, if you so wish.

5) Click "Enter".

6) Proceed on the formula tab and in the formula Auditing group, press "Show Formula". The formula in cell A1 shows.

7) Press "Show Formulas" again to turn off formula display.

8) Save the workbook in your Excel lesson 4 folder as "04 formula exercise session".

Now what is a formula in Excel? This is an equation that performs calculations, such as additions, multiplication, division and subtraction on values in a worksheet. In Excel, a value can be either a cell address, a date, text, number or Boolean data but most times is usually a number of cell address in terms of formulas.

A formula contains two elements and they are; calculation operators and operands. Operands signify the values to be used in calculation. An operand can either be a constant value or a variable such as a cell reference, another formula or a range of cells.

A constant is a text or number value that is entered directly into the formula. A variable is a name or sign that represents or identifies something else, which can be range of cells, cell address and it goes on and on. Calculation operators indicate the calculations to be performed, so as to allow Excel differentiate formulas from data, and all formulas begin with an equal sign (=)

PS: You can either start a formula with either a minus (-) or a plus (+) symbol. This serves as the beginning calculation operator, but with Excel it changes to an equal symbol when you click "Enter". Excel does not recognize or operate like 5+6=, it negates this, treating it like an ordinary string of characters.

Excel uses four kinds of calculation operators and they are; comparison, text concatenation, reference and arithmetic.

When building a formula it shows in the formula bar and in the cell itself. When fully completing a formula, and clicking "Enter" the value shows in the cell and the formula shows in the formula bar if you choose the cell. You can either edit a formula in the cell or in the formula bar, just the same way you edit any data entry.

How to Understand Order of Operators

As a user if you use above one operator in a formula, Excel would have to follow a specific order, which is called "the Order of Operations" so as to calculate the formula. Parentheses also play a fundamental role in controlling the order of operations.

Here are the steps;

Before the exercise, make sure to use the worksheet from the previous exercise.

1) Press cell A1 to make it an active cell.
2) Press in the formula bar.
3) Insert parentheses around the number your working with, for example 7+8.
4) Insert parentheses around 3/2.
5) Insert parentheses around (7+8) * (3/2).
6) Save the workbook in your Excel Lesson 4 fold as "05 Order of Operations Solutions".

Excel most of the times do apply the rules of mathematics so as to determine how formulas are calculated. The following is the order in which arithmetic operators applies;

- Percent (%)

- Negative number(-)
- Addition (+) and subtraction(-) (left to right)
- Multiplication (*) and division(/) (left to right)

For example; 7+8*3/2-4=15

According to arithmetic operator principles or priorities, the 1st operation is 8 multiplied by 3 and the result is divided by 2. Then 7 is added and 4 is subtracted.

You also have the liberty to use parentheses in a formula, which overrides the standard of operations. Excel operates with parentheses by performing the needed calculation and parentheses inside of parentheses are called "Nested parentheses". Such calculations are done on formulas in the innermost group of parentheses first of all, and from left to right if nested parentheses are at the same level. Therefore the result of the succeeding formula with parentheses is wholly different from the previous one.

$((7 + 8) * (3/2)) - 4 = 18.5$

With these arithmetic operator principles, the 1st operation is the sum of 7 + 8 which is multiplied by the operation of 3 divided by 2. Then 4 is eventually subtracted.

PS: Perhaps you may wish to revert back to the former formula while modifying a complex formula. All you have to do is click the "Esc" button on your keyboard. And if you've already pressed "Enter", you'll also have to press the "Undo" button on the Quick Access Toolbar.

Applying Cell References in Formulas

A cell reference identifies a cells spot or location in the worksheet, which is based on its column row number and letter. Applying a cell reference in contrast to the data shown in a cell permits the user to have more flexibility in his or her worksheet. If the data in a cell change, any formula that also reference the cell changes as well.

Like for example, if cell E1 consists of numbers 12 but is later changed to 15, at such a point any formula that makes reference of cell E1 updates automatically. The same principle also applies to a cell that contains a formula and

COUNTIF		X ✓	f_x	=B5*C5		
A	B	C	D	E	F	G
1 Product	Quantity	Price	Amount			
2 bread	2	1.5	3			
3 butter	1	1.2	1.2			
4 cheese	3	2	6			
5 ham	3	1.8	=B5*C5			
6						

is referenced in another formula.

How to use relative cell reference in a given formula

First question before proceeding, what is relative cell reference? This is one that adjusts the cell identifier automatically, especially if you insert or delete column or rows, or of you copy the formula to another cell. This is a kind of formula whose reference change relatively to the location where it is moved or copied.

Applying relative Cell reference in a formula

Open file, *05 budget cell reference* and proceed

1) Press cell B18
2) Press the formula bar and replace 1200 with B3 or if you have a number your working with you can still follow the instructions. You'll observe that cell B3 is highlighted and surrounded by a blue border, while you modify the formula.
3) Click "Enter". The formula in cell B18 now uses a relative cell reference to cell B3.
4) Now copy cell B18 to cell B21. The shown result changes to 400.

5) You'll observe in the formula bar that the formula cell B21 is =B6 + 500 -100, but the formula you had copied is =B3 + 500-100. That's because the original cell reference of cell B3 had changed to cell B6 when you had copied the formula down 3 cells and cell B6 is blank. The cell reference would have to be adjusted relative to its position in the worksheet.

6) Another way to use cell reference is to press the cell being referenced while making or modifying formula. Cell B21 being still active, press the formula bar and choose B6.

7) Press cell B3 and cell B3 becomes highlighted and surrounded by a blue dashed border, and the cell B3 shows in the formula bar rather than cell B6, click "Enter".

8) Save the workbook in Excel Lesson 4 folder as *05 budget cell reference solution.*

You can only use relative cell references when you want to automatically adjust or fill the formula across down columns or rows in ranges of cells. And by default, new formulas in Excel use relative references.

You can also make reference to a range of cells in a given formula. Cell referencing is one important aspect in Excel. It is unlike solving mathematics on a piece of paper (which is often arranged in columns or single rows), and more of non-adjacent, creating formulas that reference cells absolutely anywhere in the worksheet.

Applying Absolute Cell Reference in a formula

Please, use worksheet as modified in the previous exercise

1) Press cell B18.

2) Press in the formula bar and insert dollar sign in the B3 cell reference so it looks more like $B$3.

3) Click "Enter" and the formula in cell B18 now applies a complete cell reference to cell B3.

4) Copy cell B18 to cell B21, and the shown result is 1600, which matches B18.

5) Copy cell B21 to cell C21 and the shown result is still 1600.

6) You'll observe in the formula bar that the cells in cells B21 and C21 are =$B$3+500-100.

7) Now save the workbook.

Price		Quantity	Total Price
$	19.96	5 $	=$D$6*$E$6
$	32.48	3 $	97.44
$	19.97	7 $	139.79
$	4.99	10 $	49.90
$	29.97	9 $	269.73

What is an absolute cell reference? This refers to specific range of cells regardless of where the formula is spotted in the worksheet. It includes 2 dollars signs in the formula, which precedes the row number and column letter. The absolute cell reference $B$3 for example always refers to column (B) and row (3). When copying the formula to any other cell in the active worksheet, the absolute reference will negate adjusting to the destination cells.

Applying mixed cell reference in a formula

Please, do use worksheet modified in the previous lesson

1) Press cell B21.
2) Click in the formula bar and remove the dollar symbol before 3 in the formula so it looks like $B3.
3) Click "Enter" and the formula in the cell B21 now uses a mixed cell reference.
4) Copy cell B21 to cell C22. The shown result is 440, which is entirely different from the result B21. And that's because the formula in C22 references cell B4. The dollar symbol before the B in the formula is absolute and the row number is relative.
5) Delete or remove contents of cell B21, cell C21 and cell C22.
6) Save the workbook.

What is a mixed cell reference? This is a cell reference that uses a complete row or column reference, and not both.

Applying cell ranges in formula

In this program a set of cells is what it called ranges. The cell groups are either non-contiguous or contiguous. The use can also name and define ranges and change the size of ranges after defining them, also going to the extent of using named ranges in formulas.

The Name Manager and Name box do help in tracking named ranges and all cell addresses. There is also the opportunity to paste names instructions or command so as to make a combined list of named ranges and their addresses in a worksheet.

How to name a range

Open data file and proceed to name *05 Budget ranges.*

1) Press "Enable content" you may be immediately prompted and seeing another message box, press "Continue" and press "Yes" if still prompted to

make the file a trusted document, press the "Expense Details" sheet tab.

2) Select B3:D14. These are cells to be named.

3) To the left of the formula bar, press the "Name Box".

4) Then proceed to type a one-word name for the list, such as "Q1Expense" and then click "Enter". With this, the range name shows in the Name Box. Excel saves this name and proceeds in using it any subsequent reference to this particular range.

5) An optional way to name a range is using "New name" task pane or dialog box. Choose B16:M16.

6) On the formula tab, right in the Defined Names group press "Define Name", and the New Name task pane shows.

7) The program uses the row heading as the range name, which is shown in the Name text box. You

can change name if you so wish. But for this particular lesson leave the default name.

8) Then you "Open "the "Scope" drop-down list. Your alternatives are Expense details, summary and Workbook. While the last 2 entries correspond directly to particular sheets in the workbook. "Close" the drop-down list, leaving the workbook chosen.

9) Type comments in comment text box, if you wish.

10) Leave the cell address that shows in the Refers to text box. This is the particular range you had chosen. You'll also observe that the sheet name is also included quickly.

11) Click "Ok". The name Utilities_Subtotals is saved for the range B16:M16.

12) A 3rd way to name a range is to use the **Create Names from selection** task pane. Choose N2:N14. This choice includes the column heading label.

13) On the formulas tab, in the Defined names group, click "Create from selection" and the **Create Names from selection** task pane is shown.

14) This program determines that you wish to use column heading label as the range name. Press "OK" and the range name is saved with the name "Total".

15) Open the Name Box drop-down list. You have 3 named ranges from which to choose.

16) Save the workbook in your Excel Lesson 4 folder as 05 Budget ranges solution.

Named Range is a set of cells and sometimes a single cell, with a designated name. The most common idea to name a range is to refer to in functions or formulas.

Naming an individual cell or ranges according to data they contain is a time-saving technique, even though sometimes it doesn't seem so, especially when you work with a limited number of data files for this lesson. Although naming a range in complex worksheet enables you to go to the location quickly, which is similar to a bookmark.

After choosing a range of cells, you can name range using 3 different ways;

o By applying the "Create Names from

A	B	C	D	E	F
Item	Start Date	January Visitors	Vistors in First Quarter	January VisitorsVistors in First Quarter	Income
Item A	9/9/2007	1	12		34 $
Item A	10/10/2007	2	11		54 $
Item C	11/11/2007	3	10		69 $
Item D	1/1/2008	4	9		68 $
Item E	2/2/2008	5	8		67 $
Item F	5/5/2006	6	7		51 $
Item G	12/12/2006	7	12		52 $
Item H	1/10/2004	8	13		53 $
Item I	10/12/2007	9	14		54 $
Item J	4/9/2009	0	15		55 $
Item K	12/1/2010	11	16		56 $
Item B	11/12/2005	2	17		57 $

selection" task pane.

o By applying the "New Name" task pane.

- By typing name in the "Name Box" which is next to the formula bar.

Here are the guidelines for naming ranges and they are as follows;

- These range names may not contain sole letters, for example, "R", "r", "c" or "C", these are used as short-cuts for choosing rows and columns.
- They can be up to 255 characters in length.
- They may not include spaces. Microsoft advises you use the underscore character(_) or period (.) to distinguish words, for instance, Personal.Budget and Fruit_List.
- These names are not the same as cell reference, such as $B$3 or A7.
- They may begin with a letter, a backlash (/), the underscore character (_). While the rest may

include periods, numbers, underscore characters, and letters, excluding a backlash.

All name range do have a scope and it's either to an entire workbook or to a specific worksheet. The *scope* of a name is the spot within that the program recognizes the name without qualification.

Excel's main requirement is that a name must be particularly unique within its scope, but you can also use the name in a variety of scopes. In the new Name task pane, if you choose worksheet name from the scope list, the scope would be at a local sheet level. And in another you choose workbook, the scope would be at a global workbook level.

Applying External Cell references

In this part, you've been modifying or making cell references that refers to cells in the same worksheet.

Albeit, you can also make reference to cells in another worksheet right in the same workbook or in another work book completely. References to cells spotted in distinct workbook are considered external references and that is unless, you indicate either another workbook or worksheet. All Excel does is assume your cell references are to cells in the active worksheet.

How to refer to data in another worksheet

Before we proceed, what is an external reference? This refers to a range or cell in a worksheet located in another Excel workbook or a defined name in another workbook.

How to refer to data in another Worksheet

Please use worksheet you modified in the previous lessons.

1) Press the "Summary" sheet tab in the **04 Budget cell reference solution** workbook.

2) Press cell D8. Do you want the average payment for electricity to show in the cell, similar to the content that shows in B20 in the expense details worksheet. Although, your formula must have a reference to the Expense details worksheet to gather all data.

3) Type =SUM ('Expense Details '! N8)/12 and click "Enter". This formula makes a division of the value of cell N8 in the Expense Details worksheet by 12. The results is 176, which is completed due to cell formatting applied to the worksheet.

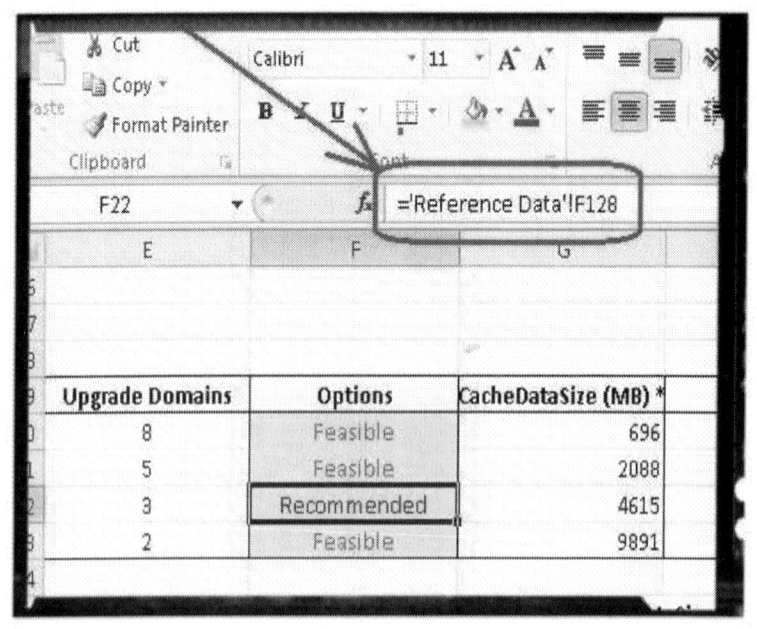

The required format of a formula that makes reference to a cell is in distinct worksheets is Sheet Name! Cell Address. This is done by entering the external worksheet name which is followed by an exclamation point, and then a cell address in the external worksheet. And that is for worksheet names that include a variety of spaces, you'll need to enclose the name in a single quotation marks, similar to 'Sheet Name'! Cell Address.

The user can also make reference to a range of cells located in an external worksheet. For instance, in the lesson, you can apply similar formula, =SUM ('Expense Details'! B8:M8)/12, to aim the same task. This formula is known to add the values in the range B8:M8 and then divides them by 12 to make the average monthly payment for electricity for more than a year.

Microsoft activates or makes a certain link reference to cells in another workbook or in another worksheet, and that's because you are basically linking data in those remote spaces or locations.

How to refer data in another workbook

Use worksheet you modified in previous lessons.

1) Proceed by opening a second workbook, which is named "04 Budget 2016".
2) Return to the previous workbook as named and on the summary sheet, press cell C3.
3) Type = ([04Budget2016.xisx] Summary! B3) and click "Enter". The formula immediately links to cell B3 on the summary sheet in the workbook named "04Budget2016".
4) Save workbook and then "Close" it.
5) Close 04Budget2016.

The paired brackets as shown in the steps above, is made so as to ease identification of name in the workbook file and Summary!, makes for identification of worksheet within the given file.

Chapter Four
Charts and pictures

In this section, we would be giving a brief on how to create charts and apply beautiful pictures on your workbook or worksheet.

Chart
Now what is a chart? A chart can be explained as a graphical representation of numeric data in a worksheet. Such data values are represented by graphs which is combined of horizontal or vertical rectangles (which can be columns or bars), lines, variety of shapes and points.

When desiring to make a chart or change an existing chart, you can select from sixteen chart types with variety of combo charts and subtypes. These could include 5 new chart types offered in Excel 29016, and they are; Box & Whisker, Waterfall, Sunburst, Histogram, and Treemap.

Below are a few description of commonly used Excel chart categories

- o Combo: These are 2 or more chart categories, such as column and line, which is depicted in a single graphic.
- o Pie: This is useful for making comparison of size of items in one data series, and how each slice would compare with the whole. Data points are shown as a percentage of a circular pie. Its arrangement is done by only one data series and none of the values are negative or zero.
- o Bar: This is useful for illustrating comparisons within individual items when an axis labels are long. Values represented here are, horizontal

rectangles. Its arrangement are done by types or time are along the vertical axis and values along the horizontal axis.

- Column: This is useful for comparing values across types or a time period. And they are vertical rectangles. Its arrangement is in any order, but still made in categories or time, they are usually on horizontal axis and values are on vertical axis.
- Bubble: This is useful for making comparison of 3 sets of value. The first value is horizontal distance, for the second value is vertical distance, and the third value is the size of the bubble.
- Area: This is useful for emphasizing magnitudes of change over time. It also displays relationships of sections or parts to the whole. Values are represented as a shaded area.

- Stock: This is useful for illustrating the fluctuation of stock prices or scientific data and when there is either a beginning end, high, and low or high value during each specified period. For each time periods, there are 3 to 5 numbers.
- Radar: this is useful for displaying variety if variables for each specified subject, which is standardized to the same scale. It presents values as points that radiate on spikes from the center. The first column is a label of spike, first row is label of units. Values for each unit go down each column starting in the second column after the row labels.
- Surface: This is useful for balanced combinations between 2 sets of data. And the resulting plot looks quite similar to a topographic map or piece

of doth draped over particular points. Both types and categories are numeric values.

- Line: This is useful for displaying trends in data at equal intervals. It shows continuous data overtime which is set against a common scale. Values are presented as points along a given line. Time is arranged in equal units on horizontal axis and values on vertical axis.

- Doughnut: This is useful for showing the relationship of sections or parts to a whole. It can also contain more than one data series. Values here are presented as sections or parts of a circular band. This can be in categories of colors arranged in circular bands and the size of the bands are the stated values of each band.

- XY (Scatter): This is useful for displaying relationships of a single numeric set of data against another numeric set of data to see if there is a relation between the two stated variables.

These charts are located above the worksheet and can be easily applied. This is done by clicking its image on the insert tab of the ribbon. More important than the chart type is the selection of the data you want to show graphically. The question that may arise when working with the worksheet is, what parts of data do you want your viewers to notice?

And there are two basic ways to identify data for your charts. If you have an efficient laid-out worksheet, you can choose a variety of ranges at one time that will eventually become the differing chart elements. The second way is identifying the chart categories and then choose the data for each chart element.

Pictures or Graphics

I guess you know placing a picture on your worksheet can hold far greater meaning than any other thing. In the case of this program, pictures are worth a thousand cells filled with number and texts. Applying photos is quite easy in Excel and all it takes is helping you take a worksheet filled with texts and numbers and transforming it into something interesting to read, easy to navigate and compelling to look at.

How to insert picture from a file

A graphic is an art-related item or object, such as an image, shape or drawing. You can use this by using the Picture button on the insert tab, it is easy and quick to add any pictures that you may have stored in your computer.

Steps

First of all, launch Excel and open a new workbook.

Download the images and files you need for this lesson and save them in the pictures folder. Or you can create a subfolder in your student folder named ***Lesson 12 drawing and images*** and proceed in saving the images in that subfolder.

1) Press or click the insert tab, then in the illustrations group, press the pictures button. The *insert picture* task pane activates or opens.

2) Navigate to the folder that holds the image files for this particular lesson. Double-click the *13 happy kid's* image or press it once and press the insert button. The picture is immediately inserted into your worksheet.

3) Now save the workbook in the Excel Lesson 13 folder as *13 insert picture solution*.

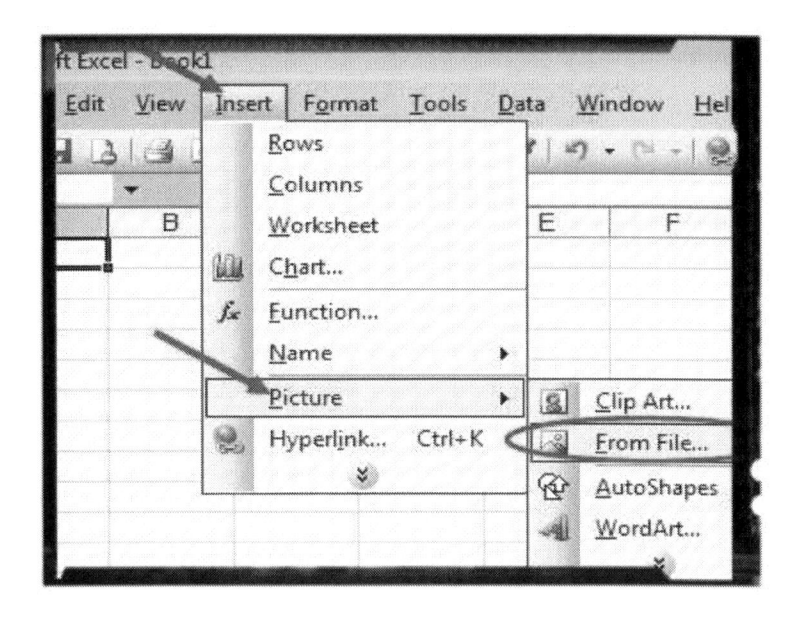

Quick resolution: Perhaps you see no picture file listed in the insert picture dialog box after navigating to your folder, in which you have your pictures stored. Well, press all pictures drop-down list located at the right of the file Name box. The program displays all picture file formats or style that it supports, such as JPG, BMP, TIFF, PNG and so much more.

Printed in Great Britain
by Amazon